The Heel of Bernadette

Colette Bryce was born in Derry in 1970 and currently lives in London. She received an Eric Gregory Award in 1995. She works as a bookseller, writer and editor.

T0331563

Colette Bryce

The Heel of Bernadette

PICADOR

First published 2000 by Picador

This edition published 2013 by Picador
an imprint of Pan Macmillan, a division of Macmillan Publishers Limited
Pan Macmillan, 20 New Wharf Road, London N1 9RR
Basingstoke and Oxford
Associated companies throughout the world
www.panmacmillan.com

ISBN 978-1-4472-4885-9

Visit **www.panmacmillan.com** to read more about all our books
and to buy them. You will also find features, author interviews and
news of any author events, and you can sign up for e-newsletters
so that you're always first to hear about our new releases.

For Mónica Castro González

Acknowledgements are due to the editors of the
following publications: *Smith's Knoll*, the *Independent*,
Arts Council Live Literature Review, *Verse* and
Poetry Review.

Some of these poems first appeared in *Anvil New Poets 2*,
edited by Carol Ann Duffy (Anvil Press, 1995).

I am grateful to The Society of Authors for an Eric
Gregory Award in 1995, to the Arvon Foundation,
and to the Tyrone Guthrie Centre at Annaghmakerrig
for a residency in 1999.

Many thanks to Kate Clanchy for her advice and
encouragement.

Contents

The Heel of Bernadette

Footings

You could see, for the life of you, no clear point
in monkeying seven, eight feet to the ground;
to slide from the belly, swing there (caught
by the arms, by the palms, by the fingertips), drop.
If I'd taken the trouble of minuses, pluses,
the length of the body, the height of the wall,
even pushed myself to prediction, scared you;
as it stood, before you leapt, I dared you.

And the lane it was yeared into two deep tracks
as we found our feet in the lengthened light,
for those with the leap approach to life,
for those who measure, look, think twice.
Both of us sobbing, I shouldered you home
with your hard-won knowledge, broken bone.

Line,

you were drawn in the voice of my mother;
not past Breslin's, don't step over.
Saturday border, breach in the slabs,
creep to the right, Line,
sidelong, crab,

cut up the tarmac, sunder the flowers,
drop like an anchor,
land in The Moor as a stringball
ravelling under the traffic,
up, you're the guttering scaling McCafferty's,

maze through the slating,
dive from sight and down into history, Line,
take flight in the chase of the fences,
leap the streets
where lines will meet you, race you, lead

you into the criss-crossed heart of the city
of lines for the glory, lines for the pity.

Break

Soldier boy, dark and tall, sat for a rest
on Crumlish's wall. *Come on over.*

Look at my Miraculous Medal.
Let me punch your bulletproof vest. *Go on, try.*

The gun on your knees is blackened metal.
Here's the place where the bullets sleep.

Here's the catch and here's the trigger.
Let me look through the eye.

Soldier, you sent me for cigs but a woman
came back and threw the money in your face.

I watched you backtrack, alter, cover
your range of vision, shoulder to shoulder.

Father, in the face

of the windscreen sun
through slow familiar roads, I've sworn
you haven't changed,
you haven't aged
an inch.

So I can't explain,
when you climb down to the lake,
what it is that makes me wait,
makes me take up the binoculars,
follow you from point of view of passenger.

Maybe it's the strange stopped nature of the day,
or something in the way
I cut the dial through distances
to focus

on what it is that shifts,
or what it is that causes
the missing years so suddenly to fall in you,
to call in me, so suddenly, this fear for you.

Lines

(for P. B.)

I have given birth to a see-through child.
In the midwife's cloth its skin cools
and sets to a delicate shell, not quite
opaque but vague like frosted glass.

Closer, I see the insides press
like noses smudged on windows,
and a web of a million arteries
bleached with a terrible absence of blood.

I don't know what to do with it.
I am trying to get back to my mother.
But the cab-driver drops it as I try to pay
and all I can do is stand here and stare

at my broken baby, spilt across the kerb –
when my sister springs from a hopscotch game,
skipping towards me, laughing. Calm down,
she says, It all fits back together, look. See?

The Pieces

Transit van, fireguard, canvas,
standard lamp, a wintered lake,
art room, lips, a baby bath,
two hands, a knife, a wedding cake,

pavement, sandals, banister,
champagne, rucksack, bus stop, ear,
sunset, ceiling, knee sock, corner,
forehead, skyline, sofa, car,

Santa Claus, cartoon, carnations,
Easter egg, Communion veil,
ocean, windows, LPs, onions,
waving painted fingernails,

breast, a mattress, transit van,
witch's cat, a threshold, ash,
eyebrow, paint-brush, bed sheet, snow-man,
foot, balloon, a black moustache,

forearm, ribbons, dinner plates,
turpentine, baptismal font,
cashpoint, paper party hats,
pumpkin, yellow plastic phone,

ambulance, red-brick houses,
pinafore, the Isle of Skye,
sand, a priest, a pair of glasses,
swimsuit, tinsel, altar, thigh.

Reading

The day you were taken to hospital
I slipped through a door to a wall of backs.
Let me tell you something.
I thought of your quietness on the phone.

A new discovery took the stand,
out from the shadows, into the light.
Hands collided with other hands,
fast, then slow, then lapsed and were quiet.

Vocal sounds took up the slack,
rising and falling, softly and steadily,
and every brick in the wall of backs
had eyes that looked at the new discovery.

Eyes that looked at the new discovery
saw every brick in a wall of backs,
rising and falling, softly and steadily.

Vocal sounds take up the slack,
fast, then slow, then lapse and are quiet.
Hands collide with other hands.

Out from the shadows, into the light,
new discoveries take the stand.
I think of your quietness on the phone.

Let me tell you something.
I slipped through a door to a wall of backs
the day you were taken to hospital.

Sister

If there was something I
or anyone could say
to show the way – the right thing –

like a track that we knew
to be clear and tried and true,
I would put it in writing.

All that filtered to mind
last night, when we found
we were tired of talking,

was the time we were lost
in that pale African fog,
and just kept walking.

My Theory

I'm watching, Rat, as you shift about,
from my upstair opposite vantage point.
You happen, large and sudden,
in someone's scrap of garden.
Part obscured by the tinder litter,
swept and stirred by the winds all winter,
Rat, you've come to prove to me
your being, your proximity,
in case I disbelieve.

I'm watching still. You skulk and freeze.
A car approaches, enters, leaves
its roar in the road between us.
And you resume your snuffling,
examining and crumpling
discarded plastic bags.
Minutes slow and limp and drag.
I wait you out, determined now
to face the tail, the teeth, the claw,

you crawl across the balding grass
to streetlight stooped across the path
and there at last you're clear to me,
not quick and sleek and cheeky –
but a portly, lumberly, punk of a shape?
Ah Hedgehog, here like an act of grace,
tonight, with thanks to you,
my theory on the absence
of the objects of my fear holds true.

Heroes

I used to side with suicides,
the solemn mail of morning tides,
hopeless railroad valentines,
the sullen youths or laughing brides
in photographs, in books, in black and white.
I used to think them heroes, brave and wise.
It's strange the way the years adjust the eyes,
the mind, to meet us, further down the line,
with heroes of another kind.

The ones that stopped, stepped back, slowed down,
have borne the time in minutes, hours,
have known the line but somehow carried on.
That girl with swimming vision
who picked up the phone.
And this man, descending the xylophone
steps from the bridge, on this worn afternoon,
who knows, may clear the journey home,
take his coat off, put the kettle on.

Itch

I believe that Jesus lives
deep in the ditch of my mother's ear,

an unreachable itch that never leaves.
And I believe when Jesus breathes

a million microscopic hairs
lean in the breeze like sapling trees.

Things I begin to tell her,
I believe sometimes she cannot hear

for the whispering like wishes
of Jesus softly breathing there.

Hit Shite and It Flies High

I have never yet met anyone with such keen ears
as the man from Moville who soberly swears
on each loose leaf of his family tree
(as traced to the deep Armada wreck
by the aunt who famously leased the shack
to the gang who launched that first attack
on the British military checkpoint,
and the worst – it is generally agreed)
that he hears the very fish at swim in the sea.

But the thing about him – despite this gift,
he works his shift and drinks his tea
modestly, like you or me.

Buster

Under a forty-watt bulb the plastic kettle bubbles
along to a scratched Patsy Cline. A swivel mirror
cranes its neck as if to catch the light, but finds
two redwebbed eyeballs, framed in a stubbled face.
Buster braves his throat to the wavering blade.

Shaved, he scuttles the stairs and out
then labours back three flights with a bagful
of jangling bottles, slots the chain to the lock.
Midnight, he shivers and thumps the fire,
whose single bar is growing dim, causing his jar

of 5p coins to suddenly shudder, suddenly ring.
Come two, he roars a toast to the coats that hang
to a human shape on the back of his door.
And he was hoovering come four, and weeping;
just cursing the way, the ups and downs of the floor.

Woman & Turkey

I needed a drink before handling it,
the clammy skin, thin and raw.
I remembered touching a dead bishop once;
Sign of the Cross, shivers.

Its feet, ditched in the sink, reached
like withered hands appealing.
The crack of its bones chilled my own.
I sank another, severed the neck.

The membranous eyes were unsettling,
the shrunken head bereft on the block,
the clutch and the squelch as innards slopped out –
gizzard, heart, lungs.

I finished the bottle to see it through
and caught the scene in the night behind glass,
a corpse like a glove to my wrist.
I am sick to the stomach of Christmas.

It's hazy then until Boxing Day,
a shock of light across the room.
I wake to blood trapped under my nails,
to the delicate snap of a wishbone.

Form

For some time I have been starving myself,
and not in the interest of fashion,
but because it is something to do
and I do it well.

I'm writing this as my only witness
has been the glass on the wall.
Someone must know what I've done
and there's no one to tell.

Commitment is the main thing. After this,
the emptiness, the hunger isn't a sacrifice
but a tool. I found I was gifted, good.
And full of my vocation, sat or stood

at the mirror just watching my work
take shape, conform to my critical eye.
Or would lie, supine, stomach shrinking,
contracting, perfecting its concave line.

Each day gave a little more: depth to the shallows
of the temples, definition to the cheek,
contrast to the clavicle, the ankle bone, the rib,
the raised X-ray perception of my feet.

But one night I dressed and went for a walk
and felt a latent contamination of eyes
from windows and cars. I'd been feeling
strange, somehow encased, the hollow rush

of my own breath like tides in the shell
of my own head. A woman passed
and I saw myself in her glance,
her expression blank as a future.

The next day I woke to double vision,
everything suddenly terribly clear, only twinned.
My hearing, too, was distracted.
I sipped some water and retched.

My speech, when I test it, has stretched
to a distant slur like a voice from behind a door.
I would think I was losing my mind
if it wasn't behind all this from the start.

Tonight there's an almost imperceptible buzzing
in my bones, like the sound of electric razors,
a lawn-mower several gardens down.
I worry that they're crumbling

under my skin, dissolving like aspirin.
I worry that my bones are caving in.
When I sit my joints begin to set.
I try to stand and I'm hit by a shift in gravity,

the point where an aircraft lifts and enters flight.
And I think my sight is burning out.
I think it is losing its pupil heart.
Objects are calmly vacating their outlines,

colours slowly absorbing the dark.
In my dream the shovels uncover a hare,
preserved in its form, its self-shaped lair,
and I'm travelling in. There is no going back.

Wish You Were

Here, an aftertaste of traffic taints
the city's breath, as mornings
yawn and bare this street

like teeth. Here, airplanes leaving
Heathrow scare this house
to trembling; these rooms protect

their space with outstretched walls,
and wait. And evenings fall
like discs in a jukebox, playing

a song called *Here*, night after night.
Wish you were. Your postcards
land in my hall like meteorites.

Phone

Though we've come to hate this line
we call; stuck evenings when we've dried
the well of talk, we bide the time
in small long-distance silences
and lend ourselves as audience
to voices washed from tense to tense
across the middle air.

So, often, more than I can bear,
missing you brings this desire
at least to hear and to be heard
and then, there's something to be said
for this. For this becomes a web,
becomes a hair, a strength, a thread,
a harness between us, in all fairness,
you in my hereness, me in your thereness.

Stars

These buildings crowd like mountains.
Here on the roof
they lapse like cliffs
to rivers of lights of the late
traffic, drowning through the streets.
Here is the distance between us.
Stars are masters of this.

You spoke of them in your letter,
how constellations overwhelm
your mountains and your river.
Here, the skies have taken cloud cover.
For us, one helicopter star.

Chapter Eight of
A Child's Companion

It was Primary Six, or possibly Seven,
but was it the day your face first reddened
to warm the room for the worst of winter's
heated attempts to shrink your head
into the depths of your knit vermilion jumper?

Was it mouthed solutions in mental arithmetic,
face like a fish until hooked by the neck
by the late, all-seeing, Sister Wimple,
or the *siss* of steam as a trusty side-kick
licked his thumb and gauged your temple;

or Chapter Eight of *A Child's Companion* –
sudden, scarlet, mortification
in Reading when you got st-stu-stuck,
and the gulp as the rough bare boards broke open
under your chair and gobbled you up?

Or was it that note I never got
in the back of my Nature Studies jotter,
all rubbed out but discernible still
by the dent of a pencil under pressure,
a patch of the page that little bit thin?

I Have

I have sat where you sit, a balancing act
on two back prongs of a straight-backed chair,

longed myself from face to feet
to a passable portrait of *taedium vitae*;

I have sympathy,
the rent to pay,

just this hour and the class next week
on the finer points of the Perfect Aspect.

If I could truly help you, give one gift,
it wouldn't be trick examination tips;

I'd grant you the power not to become
those people you despised while young.

The Apprentices, Interior Derecha

Each on the hour, main door swinging
shut on the monotone drone of the city,
students of singing – building and digging
above and below that one dull note
to which, on the hour, they step back out.

Voices are climbing, rung by rung,
the opposite lines of washing, strung
at our windows; second, third floor, high,
chasing that square of communal sky
then returning, only to try and try.

Hour upon hour this practising scales
in heartbreaking repetition,
while you sit working the notes of a line
of words that will later fail.
This is the sound of all aspiration.

Young

Loose stacks of cassettes collapse
to the slam of the door behind us.
We take the stairs
in twos and threes,

we don't know where we might be
this time next year,
but meanwhile,
we apply to the future in lunch-breaks;

taste the possibility, the sweet adhesive
strip of A4 envelopes on tongues,
punch the day and run
to post, to home, and out.

We eye each other up as future lovers;
our faces smooth as blank maps
of undiscovered countries,
where only we might go.

We mean to go, we thumb the guides,
we spin the globe and halt it
at Calcutta, then Alaska, now Japan,
and plan. Imagine.

Not for us the paper lanterns of remember,
but the hard bright bulbs of sheer want.
We reminisce at length
about the future, which is better;

we harbour it in our hearts
like a terrible crush. We laugh
and drink to this in rented rooms.
We think Not this, but older, elsewhere, soon.

Epilogue

The journey back was a nightmare.
Alice was menstrual, resentful,
complaining she always has to drive;
she was gripping the wheel at arm's length
as though appalled, repelled,
as we ripped through a sprawled
and sleeping landscape into the sky.
She seemed to be lost in a half-trance
of remembering, when the car tensed –

and the white rabbit in Alice's eye
was a stark black stare in the fast lane,
pulped by a tyre on the passenger side,
sending a shudder up through the bodywork.
I screamed, and Alice's knuckles gleamed
on the steering wheel, bright with shock,
till we finally stopped so I could be sick
on the motorway roadside grass. It was too late,
Alice whispered, We were going too fast.

Wine

The corkscrew lifts its elegant arms
like the Pope greeting tourists
on his balcony. Tonight we drink

religiously, fill to a shivering inch
of the brink, carefully, almost
warily. Tonight I drink to you,

and you to me, but this time,
seriously; as if following, word
for word in the clink, a ceremony.

Plot Summary, Scene 4

Then, I would meet you again
and would greet you in fifteen different languages,
like the Pope;
approach you in a cool embrace and kiss
alternate zones of your face, solemnly, like a delegate
from some forgotten independent state
whose population wait, have staked on this
all hope.

I would talk like the rattle of chairs
across a monumental marble hall
where throngs have all stood up to toast your cause.
I would lead the applause.
And we would sign on the dotted line
come nightfall. And together,
turn and smile for the blinding flashbulbs.

Every Winged Fowl of the Air

We wake to a world invisibly tangled up in threads
of gypsy bells, to high speed helium chitter-chatter,
talk of cha-cha, ju-ju charms; each leaf discussed,
each blade of grass, with sometimes this or that
pooh-poohed, and questions asked – *Who he, who he?*
It's you, it's you, it's you, it's you.
From twigs and branches, rude wolf whistles,
missiles from computer wars and the rat-a-tat-tat
of football rattles, donkey honk of bicycle horns,
the chink-to-chink of delicate glasses, clatter of crockery
cleared away and the shrieks of children's breathless
laughter squared in a playground's break-time play
where, amid the squeaks of plastic toys, head inclined
to a thoughtful angle, faultlessly, the smallest boy
chimes the points of time on a new triangle.

Day

That was the day that went too far
and missed the turn on the Creeslough Road.
Inside our camera of car
we filmed the minutes blur and fly
the other way, towards the sky,
and stopped to watch a man extend
some paint along a stretch of fence
to six lines of slanted gate,
the colour of the passing time,
a mix of his, and yours, and mine.

Lake

That was the day with a path laid through it
down to the slippery shore of a lake,
a path we took and knew it all
as it should be under the eye of fate;
the weight of an evening's hill reflected
full in the upturned paperweight
(the million silver fish set in it,
years ago, are still embedded);
three flat stones and a chip of slate
skipped off it, just to illustrate.

Departure, Spanish Irish Time

All night we've breathed and breathed the minutes
in and out, our bones unfurled
in flat out lines like the times of our births,
nine fifteen
and a quarter to three;

now you're up first by the day blue window,
stretching, tall as six o'clock –
you say it is, but cypresses
in the distance waver, still insist
it's five to, or five past

to Marta, loading the boot of the car
for all the world like *seis y cuarto*.

Song of the Vagrant

(after the Spanish)

I have no ties here, not even you –
you who gave me your kiss when a kiss
could have killed me.
I survived.
These streets will lead to highways, water, sky.

I will see other cities through other eyes.
Another capricious mouth may kiss,
may kill me.
This is lies.
I walk these streets repeated; tethered, tied.

Cabo de São Vicente

Today, we will walk to the end of the world.
We kiss, and start the distance –
three days rested in a gale-stripped village,
one drink taken at the Last Chance Saloon.
Loves of our lives, we are blessed, convinced.
We have water and food, a known significance.

But who is this woman, rucksack-laden,
just up ahead, or tripping our heels,
stumbling on rocks in her flip-flop sandals,
sorry to bother us, wanting a match,
traipsing the cut of the sand-soft cliff,
wrestling a map in the high, high wind?

Griffon

We queue at the valley's screened enclosure,
take our places, pay a price, a scatter of coins
apiece for this; for you, a mash of blood and flesh,
a metal pail, a tethered foot, a note on natural habitat,
a roaring anger in your gut that keeps you lunging
from your rope, upward, to your element.

A whistle shrieks
and you release your vast scaffolding of wings,
perform a weighted, awkward flight, a single beat
from A to B, then low across our cowered heads
to A. You earn your piece of meat, regard us
with an ancient eye. Up there, a pencilled sketch
of peaks, eternity of sky, a far cry.

The Praying Poplars,
Easter Saturday

After another week of gales
and still in winter's stark undress,
your reaching lines in parallels
stand more and more traversed with the cross
and criss of the storm- and domino-felled.

Last night, again, one of your number,
caught by the neck by a crashing pine's
toppled weight of solid timber,
was brought, quick, to the sodden ground
but kept its footing, arched its spine
to a bow, a flip gymnastic arc,
and stuck, taut, a catapult
now wracked with agonies of sound
of split and crack in straining tendon.

You gauge the wind in nervous creaks
and, all the while, attempt to shake
a black thought from your high minds:
a bird, fraught, in a ricochet.
You meet, consult in a scratch of branches,
start your slow ecstatic sway,
your tilt to tilt in lofty columns,
holy souls, this holy day,
standing ever tall among the fallen.

The Heel of Bernadette

Love, in these, the darkest days,
I think us back to an ancient place
where the slow child, a small knelt figure,
gazes up towards another;

think if I could lead you under,
enter through that ruined gate,
I'd stand with you among the others,
lean to where a single limb,

one touch of imagined skin,
is reached over railings, rubbed and worn
to the smooth stone, as if to the bone,
by losses, wishes, mute petitions:

forehead, sternum, yoke of shoulders,
Holy Spirit, Son and Father
help us, now we're farther, older,
find in ourselves the child believer.

Nevers

Passions never spoken,
never broken but preserved,
never layered under marriages
or burnt to dust by fast affairs
are saints to us,

the sacred ones,
bodily enshrined
to lie in state like Bernadette
at Nevers of the mind;
amazing, garlanded and fair.

Older, at the inkling
of an accent or a smile,
we travel there.